presets

T0353299

The World Premiere

BARROW HILL

by Jane Wainwright

FINBOROUGH | THEATRE

First performance at the Finborough Theatre: Sunday, 19 August 2012

This production is supported by
Carol Slavid and Sofie Mason of OffWestEnd.com

OFFWESTEND.COM

BARROW HILL

by Jane Wainwright

Cast in order of appearance

Boy	**Tom Spink**
Girl	**Sarah Ridgeway**
Kath Bilby	**Janet Henfrey**
Graham Bilby	**Charlie Roe**
Alison Bilby	**Cath Whitefield**
Lucasz Wozniac	**Mark Weinman**

The play is set on the site of the old Methodist Chapel in Barrow Hill, Derbyshire, the present.

The performance lasts approximately ninety minutes.

There will be no interval.

Director	**Abbey Wright**
Designer	**Natalie Moggridge**
Lighting Design	**Miguel Vicente**
Sound Design and Original Composition	**Max Pappenheim**
Assistant Director	**Susan Crothers**
Stage Manager	**Amy Slater**
Assistant Stage Manager	**Lucy Badminton**

Our patrons are respectfully reminded that, in this intimate theatre, any noise such as rustling programmes, talking or the ringing of mobile phones may distract the actors and your fellow audience members.

We regret there is no admittance or re-admittance to the auditorium whilst the performance is in progress.

Barrow Hill is performed in repertoire and on the set of *Cornelius*, designed by David Woodhead, which plays Tuesday to Saturday evenings, and Saturday and Sunday matinees, until 8 September 2012.

Janet Henfrey | Kath Bilby
Theatre includes *Autobiographer* (Tour and Toynbee Studios), *Charged* (Soho Theatre), *All's Well That Ends Well* (National Theatre), *Tons of Money* (Theatre Royal Windsor and National Tour), *The Black Rider* (Barbican Theatre and International Tour), *Separate Tables* (for which she won the *Manchester Evening News* award for Best Supporting Actress), *The Happiest Days of Your Life* and *Tartuffe* (Royal Exchange Theatre, Manchester), *Perfect Days* (Royal Exchange Theatre, Manchester, and Watford Palace Theatre), *Orpheus Descending* (Donmar Warehouse), *Lettice and Lovage* (West Yorkshire Playhouse), *Richard III* (Haymarket Theatre, Leicester), *The Canterbury Tales* (Gielgud Theatre), *Candide* (Gate Theatre), *Medea* (Wyndham's Theatre and Broadway), *Trelawny of the Wells* (Yvonne Arnaud Theatre, Guildford, and West End), *The Rules of The Game* (Almeida Theatre), *The Good Person of Szechwan* (National Theatre), *Too Clever By Half* and *Andromache* (The Old Vic), *Lloyd George Knew My Father* (Savoy Theatre), *The Dresser* (Queen's Theatre), *Salonika* (Everyman Theatre, Liverpool), *Turkey Time* (Bristol Old Vic), *Man and Superman* (Savoy Theatre), *Ella* (ICA), *Zigomania* (Bush Theatre), *Hans Christian Anderson* (National Tour), *Mother Courage and her Children* (Paris), *Great Expectations* (Wolsey Theatre, Ipswich), *The Good Woman of Szechwan, The Madwoman of Chaillot* and *Dr Knock* (Oxford). Theatre with the Royal Shakespeare Company includes *The Merry Wives of Windsor, The Winter's Tale, Pericles, The Two Gentleman of Verona, Major Barbara* and *Bewitched.*
Film includes *Les Misérables, Jiltin Joe, Dual Balls, Dragonworld, A Pin for the Butterfly, The Tamarind Seed, Reds, Mark Gertler, The Cook The Thief His Wife and Her Lover, She'll be Wearing Pink Pyjamas, Lady Jane Grey, Handel* and *Foreign Body.*
Television includes playing Mrs Bale in seven series of *As Time Goes By*, the Teacher in *The Singing Detective*, as well as *Tipping the Velvet, The Worst Witch, The Prince*

and the Pauper, No Bananas, One Foot in the Grave, Alice in Wonderland, Simon and the Witch, Dr Who, Stand Up Nigel Barton, Unfair Exchanges, Weather in the Street, Wood and Walters, Uncle Silas, The Treasure Seekers, The Famous Five, Fatal Obsession, Boon, The Jewel in the Crown and Chocky.

Sarah Ridgeway | Girl
Theatre includes *You Can't Take It With You* (Royal Exchange Theatre, Manchester), *Sucker Punch* (Royal Court Theatre), *Days of Significance* (Royal Shakespeare Company), *The Comedy of Errors* (Shakespeare's Globe), *A Taste of Honey* (Salisbury Playhouse) and *Romeo and Juliet* (Northern Broadsides).
Television includes *Holby City*, *Call The Midwife*, *Kerry and Lu's Taster*, *Satisfaction*, *The Suspicions of Mr Whicher*, *Crimson Petal and the White*, *Doctors*, *Miss Marple*, *The Bill*, *EastEnders* and *Doctors*.

Charlie Roe | Graham Bilby
At the Finborough Theatre, Charlie appeared in *Enduring Freedom* (2008) and *The Potting Shed* (2010 and 2011). Theatre includes *A Few Good Men* (Theatre Royal Haymarket), *Educating Rita* (English Theatre Frankfurt), *The Day After the Fair* (Lyric Theatre), *Electra* (Gate Theatre), *The Taming of the Shrew*, *Rosencrantz and Guildenstern are Dead* (English Touring Theatre), *The Tempest* (Cheek by Jowl), *Macbeth*, *Waiting for Godot* (Lyric Theatre, Belfast), *As You Like It*, *Six Characters in Search of an Author*, *Ting Tang Mine* (National Theatre), *The Lady's Not for Burning* (Chichester Festival Theatre), *Troilus and Cressida* (Royal Shakespeare Company), *A Month in the Country* (Leatherhead Theatre) and *To Kill A Mockingbird* (Courtyard Theatre, Leeds and UK Tour).
Television includes *Lewis*, *Holby City*, *Ashes to Ashes*, *Derailed*, *If*, *Wire in the Blood*, *The Lakes*, *Peak Practice*, *Kavanagh QC*, *Silent Witness*, *Inspector Morse*, *Minder*, *Shackleton* and *Brideshead Revisited*.

Tom Spink | Boy
Theatre includes *South Downs* (Harold Pinter Theatre).
Film includes *Harry Potter and the Deathly Hallows.*
Television includes *Casualty.*

Mark Weinman | Lucasz Wozniac
Trained at the University of Manchester.
Theatre includes *The Hairy Ape* (Southwark Playhouse), *Captain Amazing* (Live Theatre, Newcastle), *Some Scary Stories* (Royal Exchange Theatre, Manchester), *Step 9 (of 12)* for which he received a nomination for Best Actor in the OffWestEnd Awards (Britannia Theatre), *Fast Burn* (KneeHigh Theatre), *Herons* (Stephen Joseph Theatre, Scarborough, and Library Theatre, Manchester), *Amphibians* (Bridewell Theatre), *Edmond* (Theatre Royal Haymarket), *The Emperor Jones* (National Theatre), *Still Killing Time* (National Youth Theatre at the Soho Theatre), *Nettles* and *Europe* (Contact Theatre, Manchester), *Pale Horse* (John Thaw Theatre) and *Scenes from Abroad* (Watford Palace Theatre).
Film includes *Waves, Shinos Show* and *This is Love.*
Television includes *Derren Brown: The Experiments.*

Cath Whitefield | Alison Bilby
Trained at École Internationale de Théâtre Jacques Lecoq, Theatre du Soleil and The State Institute of Theatrical Art, Moscow.
Theatre includes *Bitch Boxer* (Soho Theatre), *The Legend of Captain Crow's Teeth* (Unicorn Theatre), *Electra, How To Be An Other Woman, The Sexual Neuroses of our Parents* (Gate Theatre, London), *Elektra* (The Young Vic), *Othello* (Royal Shakespeare Company), *Between Dog and Wolf* (Paines Plough), *The Caucasian Chalk Circle* (Filter and National Theatre), *Mancub, Gobbo,* and *Home* for which she received a nomination for Best Actress in the Scottish Critics Awards

(National Theatre of Scotland), *Charlotte's Web* (Citizen's Theatre, Glasgow), *Lost Ones* (Vanishing Point Theatre), *A State of Grace* (King's Head Theatre), *Platform* (ICA), *Mother Courage* (Watford Palace Theatre), *Grid Iron* which won the award for The Best Ensemble in The Stage Awards (Fierce), *Earth* (Perdu Theatre, Amsterdam), *Sara*, *Decomposition*, *Princess Ivona*, *Into the Woods* and *Trial By Jury* (Paris), *Don Quixote* (Festival France), *The Song of Love and Death of Christopher Rilke* (National Theatre Campage), *The Resistible Rise of Arturo Ui* (National Tour), *Les Quatre Morts de Marie* and *Cabaret Flottant* (Aria Festival Corsica), *Metamorphosis* (National Tour), *First Love* (Maddermarket Theatre, Norwich), *Kingfisherbreastbone* (Brockley Jack Theatre), *Transient Blues* (Tristan Bates Theatre), *Julia* (Germany and Poland Tour), *All The World's a Biscuit* and *The Bald Prima Donna* (Edinburgh Festival), *The Government Inspector* (National Tour) and *Yerma* (Donald Roy Theatre, Hull).
Film includes *Hell's Pavement*.
Television includes *Above Suspicion: The Red Dahlia* and *The Bill*.

Jane Wainwright | Playwright

Jane was born in Derbyshire. She was a member of the Royal Court Theatre's Young Writers Programme, their Invitation Group for Playwrights and their 'Supergroup' of twelve specially selected writers. Plays include *Photos of You Sleeping* (Hampstead Theatre – Start Night), *Barrow Hill*, performed as part of *Vibrant – An Anniversary Festival of Finborough Playwrights* (Finborough Theatre), *In World*, performed as part of *Vibrant – A Festival of Finborough Playwrights* (Finbrough Theatre), *Hands Free*, part of *'AVE IT!*, in the *Coming Up Later* season (The Old Vic Tunnels) and *Pet's Corner* (The Miniaturists at the Arcola Theatre). She was shortlisted for the WritersRoom 10 scheme and the BBC Heartlands new writing scheme, and her play *In World* was part of the final shortlist in last year's PapaTango New Writing Competition. Jane is 'fostered' by OffWestEnd.com's Adopt A Playwright Award.

Abbey Wright | Director

Abbey has directed a string of critically acclaimed productions including *Bitch Boxer* (Soho), *Dublin Carol* (Donmar Warehouse at Trafalgar Studios), *Sixty-Six Books* (Bush), *Rose* (Pleasance Forth, Edinburgh), *Lakeboat* and *Prairie du Chien* by David Mamet (Arcola Theatre), *The Occupied Times* (Arcola Theatre), *National Theatre Connections 2012* (National Theatre), *The Song of Deborah* (The Lowry, Manchester), *Hidden Glory* (The Lowry, Manchester, and Tour), *The Ones That Flutter* (Theatre503), *Restoration Sketch Show* (Theatre Royal Haymarket) and *The Gay Man's Guide* (The Drill Hall). Abbey was Resident Assistant Director at the Donmar Warehouse from 2008-09, during which time she worked with such notable directors as Michael Grandage, Alan Rickman, Jeremy Herrin, Peter Gill, Sean Holmes, Jamie Lloyd and John Tiffany. She was Staff Director to Danny Boyle on *Frankenstein* at the National Theatre in 2010-11.

Natalie Moggridge | Designer
Trained at Motley and Arts Institute Bournemouth.
Theatre includes *Chelsea Hotel* (RADA), *Little Women*
(Lost Theatre), *Sixty-Six Books* (Bush Theatre), *I Still
Get Excited When I See a Ladybird* (Theatre503), *Ein
Abend Met Ruby* (Battersea Barge, Jermyn Street
Theatre and Riverside Studios), *Three Chekhov Farces*
(Arts Educational Schools), *Alfie* (Baron's Court) and
They Shoot Horses Don't They? (Pavilion Ballroom,
Bournemouth). Television and Film includes *The Charles
Dickens Show* and *Stanley Pickle.* Awards include the
2011 Distinctive Achievement for Costume Design
(Independent Wild Rose Film Festival, USA).

Miguel Vincente | Lighting Designer
At the Finborough Theatre, Miguel was Lighting Designer
for *Through the Night* (2011), *Autumn Fire* (2012), *Merrie
England* (2012) and *The Fear of Breathing* (2012).
Trained at the London Academy of Music and Dramatic
Art. Designs include *Missing* (Tristan Bates Theatre),
Normal? (Oval House Theatre), *Miss Julie* (Theatro
Technis), *The Happy Prince* (Little Angel Theatre) and
Chapel Street (Old Red Lion Theatre). Other credits
include *Kindertransport*, *The Last Days of Judas Iscariot*
and *Hedda Gabler* (Linbury Studio Theatre at LAMDA).

Max Pappenheim | Sound Designer and Original
Composition
At the Finborough Theatre, Max designed the sound for
The Fear of Breathing (2012) and directed *Perchance to
Dream* (2011).
Sound Designs include *Borderland*, *Kafka v
Kafka* (Brockley Jack Studio Theatre), *Being Tommy
Cooper* (Old Red Lion Theatre), *Four Corners One Heart*
(Theatre503), *Tangent* (New Diorama Theatre) and
Werther's Sorrows and *Salome* (Edinburgh Festival).
Directing includes *San Giuda* (Southwark Cathedral), *The
Charmed Life* (King's Head Theatre), *Finchley
Road* (LOST Theatre) and *Quid Pro Quo* (Riverside
Studios). Max was nominated for an OffWestEnd Award
2012 for Best Sound Design.

Susan Crothers | Assistant Director
Trained at East 15 and with Di Trevis.
As a director, Susan has worked with The Collective, The Suitcase Cabaret, The Feral Pigeons, Particular Theatre and most recently directed *Under the Sofa* by Tim Price and her own play, *Nice Girl* (Pick'n'Mix Festival at the New Mac, Belfast). As a writer, Susan's work has been performed at The Pleasance Islington (Graft Playwrights' Collective), the Arcola Theatre (Miniaturists season), The Spoken Space and with Tamasha at the Graeae Studios. She is a Tamasha 2012 developing writer and is currently working on the Greyscale play development programme.

India Pool | Assistant Producer
At the Finborough Theatre, India is Resident Assistant Producer on attachment from the MA in Creative Producing at Birkbeck, University of London. She is currently Associate Producer on *Hindle Wakes*.
Trained in Drama, Theatre and Performance Studies from Roehampton University. She has also worked alongside the Marketing Department at Whitechurch Securities Limited, shadowed the producer Sarah Clews at People Show, and assisted producer Leonora Wood on *The Tempest* (BITE Festival, Barbican).

SNAPDRAGON PRODUCTIONS

Executive Producer | **Sarah Loader**
Artistic Director | **Eleanor Rhode**
Business Director | **Pelham Olive**

Snapdragon Productions was formed by Artistic Director Eleanor Rhode and Producer Sarah Loader in 2009 and became a limited company under the direction of Pelham Olive in January 2012. Their productions include the London premiere of Michael Healey's *The Drawer Boy* which was named Time Out's Critics' Choice; the European premiere of Michael Healey's *Generous* (Finborough Theatre) which enjoyed two sell-out runs and was also named Time Out's Critics' Choice; the award-winning European premiere of Rodgers and Hammerstein's musical *Me and Juliet* (Finborough Theatre); *Anna Karenina* (Arcola Theatre); and a co-production of the world premiere of Anders Lustgarten's *A Day at the Racists* (Finborough Theatre and the Broadway Theatre, Barking) which was nominated for the 2010 TMA Award for Outstanding Achievement in Regional Theatre and won the playwright the Inaugural Harold Pinter Award for Playwriting. Forthcoming productions include the first London revival in over thirty years of Hugh Leonard's *A Life* at the Finborough Theatre in October 2012.
www.snapdragonproductions.com

Forthcoming Productions

A Life
by Hugh Leonard
Finborough Theatre
2 – 27 October 2012

Production Acknowledgements
Stage Manager | **Amy Slater**
Assistant Stage Manager | **Lucy Badminton**
Production Images | **Ben Broomfield**
Graphic Designer | **Rebecca Maltby**
Production Accountant | **Victoria Tills**
Image Copyright | **Gareth Wonfor**

Special Thanks to
The Workspace Group, Great Guildford Square, Ideas Tap.

 Snapdragon Productions is grateful to Ideas
Tap for providing office space through the
Ideas Tap Creative Space programme.

Snapdragon Productions Ltd. is a registered limited company.
Registered company number: 7923298. Registered office: Brook
Henderson House, 37-43 Blagrave Street, Reading, RG1 1PZ

FINBOROUGH | THEATRE

Founded in 1980, the multi-award-winning Finborough Theatre presents plays and music theatre, concentrated exclusively on new writing and genuine rediscoveries from the 19th and 20th centuries. We aim to offer a stimulating and inclusive programme, appealing to theatregoers of all ages and from a broad spectrum of the population. Behind the scenes, we continue to discover and develop a new generation of theatre makers – through our vibrant Literary team, our internship programme, our Resident Assistant Director Programme, and our partnership with the National Theatre Studio providing a bursary for Emerging Directors.

Despite remaining completely unsubsidised, the Finborough Theatre has an unparalleled track record of attracting the finest creative talent, as well as discovering new playwrights who go on to become leading voices in British theatre. Under

Artistic Director Neil McPherson, it has discovered some of the UK's most exciting new playwrights including Laura Wade, James Graham, Mike Bartlett, Sarah Grochala, Jack Thorne, Simon Vinnicombe, Alexandra Wood, Al Smith, Nicholas de Jongh and Anders Lustgarten.

Artists working at the theatre in the 1980s included Clive Barker, Rory Bremner, Nica Burns, Kathy Burke, Ken Campbell, Jane Horrocks and Claire Dowie. In the 1990s, the Finborough Theatre became known for new writing including Naomi Wallace's first play *The War Boys*; Rachel Weisz in David Farr's *Neville Southall's Washbag*; four plays by Anthony Neilson including *Penetrator* and *The Censor*, both of which transferred to the Royal Court Theatre; and new plays by Richard Bean, Lucinda Coxon, David Eldridge, Tony Marchant, Mark Ravenhill and Phil Willmott. New writing development included a number of works that went on to become modern classics including Mark Ravenhill's *Shopping and F***king*, Conor McPherson's *This Lime Tree Bower*, Naomi Wallace's *Slaughter City* and Martin McDonagh's *The Pillowman.*

Since 2000, new British plays have included Laura Wade's London debut *Young Emma*, commissioned for the Finborough Theatre; James Graham's *Albert's Boy* with Victor Spinetti; Sarah Grochala's *S27*; Peter Nichols' *Lingua Franca*, which transferred Off-Broadway; and West End transfers for Joy Wilkinson's *Fair*; Nicholas de Jongh's *Plague Over England*; and Jack Thorne's *Fanny and Faggot*. The late Miriam Karlin made her last stage appearance in *Many Roads to Paradise* in 2008. Many of the Finborough Theatre's new plays have been published and are on sale from our website.

UK premieres of foreign plays have included Brad Fraser's *Wolfboy*; Lanford Wilson's *Sympathetic Magic*; Larry Kramer's *The Destiny of Me*; Tennessee Williams' *Something Cloudy, Something Clear*; the English premiere of Robert McLellan's Scots language classic, *Jamie the Saxt*; and three West End transfers – Frank McGuinness' *Gates of Gold* with William Gaunt and John Bennett, Joe DiPietro's *F***ing Men* and Craig Higginson's *Dream of the Dog* with Dame Janet Suzman.

Rediscoveries of neglected work have included the first London revivals of Rolf Hochhuth's *Soldiers* and *The Representative*; both parts of Keith Dewhurst's *Lark Rise to Candleford*; *The Women's War*, an evening of original suffragette plays; *Etta Jenks* with Clarke Peters and Daniela Nardini; Noël Coward's first play, *The Rat Trap*; Charles Wood's *Jingo* with Susannah Harker; Emlyn Williams' *Accolade* with Aden Gillett and Graham Seed; and Lennox Robinson's *Drama at Inish* with Celia Imrie and Paul O'Grady.

Music Theatre has included the new (premieres from Grant Olding, Charles Miller, Michael John LaChuisa, Adam Guettel, Andrew Lippa and Adam Gwon's *Ordinary Days* which transferred to the West End) and the old (the UK premiere of Rodgers and Hammerstein's *State Fair* which also transferred to the West End, and the acclaimed Celebrating British Music Theatre series, reviving forgotten British musicals including *Gay's The Word* by Ivor Novello with Sophie-Louise Dann, Helena Blackman and Elizabeth Seal.

The Finborough Theatre won *The Stage* Fringe Theatre of the Year Award in 2011, won *London Theatre Reviews'* Empty Space Peter Brook Award in 2010, the Empty Space Peter Brook Award's Dan Crawford Pub Theatre Award in 2005 and 2008, the Empty Space Peter Brook Mark Marvin Award in 2004, four awards in the inaugural 2011 OffWestEnd Awards and swept the board with eight awards at the 2012 OffWestEnd Awards including Best Artistic Director and Best Director for the second year running. *Accolade* was named Best Fringe Show of 2011 by *Time Out*. It is the only unsubsidised theatre to be awarded the Pearson Playwriting Award bursary for writers Chris Lee in 2000, Laura Wade in 2005 for James Graham in 2006, for Al Smith in 2007, for Anders Lustgarten in 2009, Simon Vinnicombe in 2010 and Dawn King in 2011. Three bursary holders (Laura Wade, James Graham and Anders Lustgarten) have also won the Catherine Johnson Award for Pearson Best Play.

www.finboroughtheatre.co.uk

The Associate Director position is supported by The National Theatre Studio's Bursary for Emerging Directors, a partnership between the National Theatre Studio and the Finborough Theatre.

The Finborough Theatre has the support of the Pearson Playwrights' Scheme. Sponsored by Pearson PLC.

The Cameron Mackintosh Resident Composer Scheme is facilitated by Mercury Musical Developments and Musical Theatre Matters

The Finborough Theatre is a member of the Independent Theatre Council, Musical Theatre Network UK and The Earl's Court Society www.earlscourtsociety.org.uk

Ecovenue is a European Regional Development Fund backed three year initiative of The Theatres Trust, aiming to improve the environmental sustainability of 48 small to medium sized performing arts spaces across London. www.ecovenue.org.uk

The Finborough Wine Café
Contact Monique Ziervogel on 020 7373 0745 or finboroughwinecafe@gmail.com

Mailing
Email admin@finboroughtheatre.co.uk or give your details to our Box Office staff to join our free email list. If you would like to be sent a free season leaflet every three months, just include your postal address and postcode.

Follow Us Online

www.facebook.com/FinboroughTheatre
www.twitter.com/finborough

Feedback
We welcome your comments, complaints and suggestions. Write to Finborough Theatre, 118 Finborough Road, London SW10 9ED or email us at admin@finboroughtheatre.co.uk

Smoking is not permitted in the auditorium and the use of cameras and recording equipment is strictly prohibited

BARROW HILL

Jane Wainwright

BARROW HILL

OBERON BOOKS
LONDON

WWW.OBERONBOOKS.COM

First published in 2012 by Oberon Books Ltd
521 Caledonian Road, London N7 9RH
Tel: +44 (0) 20 7607 3637 / Fax: +44 (0) 20 7607 3629
e-mail: info@oberonbooks.com
www.oberonbooks.com

A catalogue record for this book is available from the British
Library.

PB ISBN: 978-1-84943-405-8
Digital ISBN: 978-1-84943-604-5

Cover image by Gareth Wonfor / Rebecca Maltby

Printed, bound and converted
by CPI Group (UK) Ltd, Croydon, CR0 4YY.

Visit www.oberonbooks.com to read more about all our books
and to buy them. You will also find features, author interviews and
news of any author events, and you can sign up for e-newsletters
so that you're always first to hear about our new releases.

For Madge
Marjorie Irene Hill 1908–1998

Barrow Hill was originally workshopped at the Finborough
Theatre by Jean Boht, Tom Knight, Selina MacDonald,
Thomas Morrison, David Nicolle, Catherine Skinner, directed
by Blanche McIntyre.

An earlier version of *Barrow Hill* was performed as a staged
reading as part of *Vibrant – An Anniversary Festival of Finborough
Playwrights* on 9 June 2010.

Boy	**Simon Darwen**
Girl	**Catherine Skinner**
Kath Bilby	**Janie Booth**
Graham Bilby	**Michael Kirk**
Alison Bilby	**Laura Freeman**
Lucasz Wozniac	**Alistair Reith**

Directed by Eleanor Rhode

This text went to press before the end of rehearsals
and so may differ slightly from the play as performed.

I would like to thank the entire cast and production teams of the current production and of the initial workshop and staged reading; Sarah Loader and Eleanor Rhode of Snapdragon Productions; Julia Mills at Berlin Associates; Van Badham and Neil McPherson at the Finborough Theatre; Leo Butler, Nic Wass and the Royal Court Theatre; Sofie Mason, Diana Jervis-Read, Carol Slavid and all at OffWestEnd.com.

Finally, thanks to Mum, Dad, Peter and Marcus, for your constant love and support, then and now.

– Jane Wainwright

Characters

in order of appearance

BOY

GIRL

KATH BILBY

GRAHAM BILBY

ALISON BILBY

LUCASZ WOZNIAC

The play is set on the site of the old Methodist Chapel
in Barrow Hill, Derbyshire, the present.

Unless otherwise stated, the Girl and Boy
are not seen or heard by any other characters.
They only respond to each other.

ONE

Barrow Hill, Derbyshire. Saturday, late morning, March.

A small wall surrounding a chapel runs across the stage. There is a space where a small gate has already been removed. The chapel is hidden behind scaffolding which is covered by coloured plastic. It has been ripped off in places. There is a large sign at the front of the chapel which reads 'Barrow Hill Methodist Chapel'. Next to it is a sign saying 'One and two-bedroom luxury apartments on sale. 40% Presold. Showroom open soon.' has been erected.

Throughout the play, the sound of occasional traffic can be heard from the nearby road.

A BOY, fifteen, and a GIRL, fifteen, sit on the scaffold. They are not together.

KATH, an eighty-four-year-old woman, is sat in front of the wall on a small fishing stool. Her handbag is on her lap. She is dressed smartly in a mauve skirt and jacket, although it is slightly too big for her and looks rather dated. She is holding a mop. It has been changed into a placard which reads 'Save Our Chapel'. It looks like a child has made it.

A long time passes. KATH rummages through her handbag to find a piece of toilet paper. She wipes her nose with it and places it up her sleeve. She looks into the distance defiantly for a long time. Lights down.

TWO

Later the same day. KATH is sat in the same position.

BOY is sat high up on the scaffolding. GIRL is doing forward rolls over one of the bottom bars. She eventually stops and sits. Throughout the scene, BOY glances down at GIRL.

GRAHAM, fifty-six, enters carrying three Morrisons bags, full of food.

GRAHAM: Nearly kicked yer bloody door down.

He drops the bags at KATH's feet.

I thought summat had happened.

KATH: *(Still looking at the sky.)* Exactly like day we had you christened.

GRAHAM: Where's yer phone? Yer didn't answer…

KATH hands GRAHAM the placard.

We've bin through this. I've said, I'll take yer t' one a' other chapels. Morning service. Evening. Whatever yer want.

Beat.

How long d'yer think yer gonna sit out 'ere?

KATH: As long as it takes.

GRAHAM: The builders don't call the shots. They're just followin' orders. Better this than it be pulled down altogether.

KATH takes out a foil parcel from her bag and starts to unwrap it.

I thought we could drop past Stavely.

KATH: What for?

GRAHAM: I heard their chapel's got a flat screen. Great big speakers.

KATH: To drown out sound a' all coughing.

GRAHAM: You'd be able to hear.

KATH: Sickly place. They've too much mucus.

GRAHAM: They've central heating.

KATH: We would've if they'd given us some money.

GRAHAM: There was only five of yer.

KATH: Only us that could stand it.

GRAHAM: And where are they now? Even Ferd's –

KATH: Dead.

Beat.

GRAHAM: A quick look. Five minutes. And if yer don't like it –

A rustling.

KATH: Moggy?

KATH finishes unwrapping the cheese sandwich and shakes it near the floor hoping to attract MOGGY, the chapel's stray cat. She makes kissing noises.

Here puss puss… Come on now…

GRAHAM: That cat eats better than I do.

The cat doesn't appear. She hands GRAHAM the sandwich.

Mum…

KATH: This is a place where people come together.

GRAHAM: Listen…

KATH: Why do they want to put walls in? Everyone sat on their own behind a closed door. When we had harvest festival there'd be hundreds of us packed in there. Not an hymn sheet between us.

GRAHAM: Deals done. Yer have t' accept it.

Beat.

Mum… I…

KATH: What do you see on that wall? I see all eight of my brothers sat there. S'like they've never left me.

GRAHAM: Yer memories aren't 'ere. They're wi' yer. In yer head.

KATH: Wait till you hit eighty-four. There's not enough room to pack all years in. And now these invisible men want to send them away till there's nowt left of any a' us.

Silence. GRAHAM takes a bite of the sandwich.

Yer should've brought another stool.

GRAHAM: I've got t' pick Linda up.

KATH: That's why you've got weight on. Allus rushin'. No time to chew your food properly.

GRAHAM: This isn't your chapel anymore, it's flats. Whoever you talk to, whoever does work, it's gonna be flats.

KATH: Such a pessimist. Yer father never was.

GRAHAM: Should've bin. He dropped dead at forty-five.

Beat.

I don't want yer comin' back 'ere.

KATH: S'been you and me shouldering Bilby name for a long time. We're one's who have to fight.

GRAHAM: Dad wouldn't hav' wanted yer sat out 'ere riskin' yer health.

KATH: He'd have wanted what was right.

Pause.

BOY sneezes. He immediately claps his hand over his mouth. GIRL jumps up and looks around. She spots BOY.

GIRL: Most folk'd call that spyin'. Shouldn't make a habit out a' doin' things like that. What's up, don't yer know how t' speak?

BOY: I've not been watchin'… I mean… I've…

GIRL: There's really nowt worse than a boy who doesn't know how t' speak proper.

BOY: ly.

GIRL: What?

BOY: There's really nowt worse than a boy who doesn't know how t' speak properly.

GIRL: I don't need advice from you thank you. And don't you be lookin' at me again. What a girl does in her own time's private.

GRAHAM: Yer comin' or not?

Beat.

Suit yourself. I'm not sittin' out 'ere catchin' pneumonia.

KATH retrieves an extra strong mint from her bag.

KATH: Graham!

KATH holds out the mint.

Helps with indigestion.

GRAHAM shakes his head and starts to exit.

Pause.

He walks back to KATH. He takes two meringues out of a bag and passes one to her. He sits on the wall.

GRAHAM: Half an hour. Then we're goin'.

They eat in silence. Lights fade.

THREE

The next day. Sunday. Early morning.

ALISON, twenty-six, is stood leaning on a sweeping brush with her eyes closed. There is a small battery operated radio cassette player, a flask and car keys balanced on the front chapel wall. A sledgehammer leans against the wall.

The radio is playing.

GRAHAM enters from inside the chapel.

GRAHAM: Alison!

She jerks awake.

Yer not gonna be much cop today.

ALISON: It's 8:30 on a Sunday. Told yer t' ask Lucasz.

GRAHAM: He's probably in same state as you.

ALISON: He never came out. Call him.

GRAHAM: Yer here now.

She starts to dial LUCASZ's number.

I'm not payin' double time.

ALISON: You're payin' it me.

Beat.

Dad!

ALISON hangs up the phone. GRAHAM turns the radio up. ALISON takes a swig of tea from the flask.

(Shouting over the radio.) Amount a' alcohol in my blood s'probably illegal for me t' be here. I'm still wearin' my pyjama top.

Pause.

Sure Mum'll love waking up t' an empty house on her birthday.

GRAHAM: Sooner we finish. Sooner we get paid.

GRAHAM's phone rings. He rejects the call.

ALISON: Yer could've at least let me sit and have breakfast. Nearly choked tryin' t' eat it in –

GRAHAM: Turn it off. Can't hear a bloody thing over you.

ALISON turns the radio down but it is still audible.

Yer not at college now.

ALISON: I haven't been for years.

GRAHAM: This is a job and I'm yer boss.

ALISON: Most bosses don't come into yer room at six a.m. on a Sunday and pull yer covers off.

GRAHAM: There's plenty of people lookin' for work.

ALISON: You've got t' be / kiddin'.

GRAHAM: / I heard yer come in. Gone three.

ALISON: It was Saturday night. You're one who said I watched too much TV.

GRAHAM: I meant go t' pictures or for a walk. Not get drunk wi' rabble round 'ere.

ALISON: I'm 'ere five days a week. Sometimes six. I've never bin late.

GRAHAM: Last week –

ALISON: Once. In eight years.

GRAHAM: I don't ask yer t' do anythin' I don't.

ALISON: *I* want a life.

GRAHAM: See. Yer get over tired an' act like this.

ALISON: Yer wouldn't know what time I got in if I had my own house.

GRAHAM: So move out.

Pause.

ALISON: Bumped into a guy from Hasland Hall last night. Another one rejectin' bright lights of Barrow Hill's kebab shops. He's worked in petrol station at Calow since school, never bin further than Mansfield… Now he's takin' an around the world trip. Whole year, starting in Australia.

GRAHAM: If he's got money.

ALISON: He's gettin' a job out there.

GRAHAM: Lucky for you you've got one right on your doorstep.

ALISON reluctantly starts sweeping again.

ALISON: I'm sweatin' booze. We could nip home. Two minutes. Give Mum her presents.

A look.

What? You did get her summat?

Beat.

Oh God.

GRAHAM: Whatever I get her's allus wrong. We've not got money t' throw away.

ALISON: I'm goin' home.

GRAHAM: We can't.

ALISON: I can. I bought a present.

GRAHAM: Best present I can giv' yer mum is stayin' away. Less mess. Less rows. Less sound of me breathin'.

ALISON watches GRAHAM.

ALISON: Go see her.

GRAHAM: Yer brother's goin' over.

ALISON: Not Mum. Gran. I'm guessin' yer 'aven't told her.

Beat.

Take her a plant.

GRAHAM: That's what I love about you Ali. Head in clouds.

ALISON: Or give contract up.

GRAHAM: Fancy livin' on street, do yer?

She shrugs.

Well yer Mum might.

ALISON: Yer could sell house, buy a campervan. Then yer could take it out wi' yer on Saturdays. Nip back every time yer want a cup of tea. Save yer a fortune. Take it on holiday yer wouldn't have t' pay for hotels.

GRAHAM: I'll let you run that past her, shall I?

ALISON: Might be romantic. Like being back in Sixties.

GRAHAM: Whatever you've heard about the Sixties we saw none of it round here. Only thing we got were traffic jams.

'Rose Garden' sang by Lynn Anderson comes on the radio.

Seventies however. Turn it up.

ALISON reluctantly turns the radio up.

Like yer mean it.

GRAHAM cranks it up loud and starts to dance to the music.

We're same you an' me.

GRAHAM starts to dance, with surprising grace, along the scaffolding.

ALISON: I hope not.

GRAHAM moves towards ALISON, singing.

GRAHAM: Come on, Ally!

ALISON: *(Laughing.)* No. Dad… Dad!

GRAHAM: Your mother used t' say I was very light on me toes. For a builder, anyroad. See yer ol' dad's still got it in him.

ALISON: I wish you hadn't.

GRAHAM: Bet yer never thought an old codger like me could –

KATH enters, holding her stool and placard.

ALISON: Gran!

ALISON snaps off the radio.

KATH: No.

Silence.

GRAHAM: We agreed yer weren't gonna come.

KATH: No. You wouldn't… You…

GRAHAM: Ali, get yer Gran a' tea.

ALISON grabs the flask and offers KATH a cup.

KATH: Not you. Not our…

GRAHAM: I was gonna tell yer –

KATH: Hoping I'd snuff it first?

Pause.

GRAHAM: If it isn't me it'll be someone else. Better than having some strange lot in there knocking it to pieces.

KATH: Bashing out our history.

GRAHAM: Yer think I want to do this? I've no choice. We haven't had a decent job for months. We need money.

KATH: *(Getting out her purse.)* How much?

GRAHAM: I'm not talkin' a tenner. We're missin' mortgage payments. I'm a nail's breadth away from losin' house.

KATH: That chapel's in our blood. It's one of us. Bilby's stick by their own.

GRAHAM: Who d'yer think I'm doin' it for?

KATH: Not me.

GRAHAM: I've got t' choose livin' over dead.

KATH: Which category do I fall in?

Pause.

GRAHAM: I'm sorry yer found out like this but like Alison said…

ALISON: What?

GRAHAM: The place was goin' to ruin.

ALISON: What do I know?

GRAHAM: At least now it'll have some use.

KATH: You were married in there. Ben and Alison christened. Tell them you've changed your mind.

GRAHAM: …

KATH: I've never asked you for anything. Even when yer father died…

GRAHAM: Don't start.

KATH: I've never taken a bean from you.

GRAHAM: After everythin' I've done? Chasin' around after yer. Ferryin' you and whole congregation and its wife. Repatched, repainted, repaired whole place one time or another. I didn't see nobody else's son doin' that.

KATH: I didn't ask you to.

GRAHAM: If I'd known yer weren't bothered I'd have stayed at home and had tea with my own bloody wife and daughter.

ALISON: I usually eat in my room anyway.

GRAHAM: I've done a damn sight more for you than anyone else.

Silence.

KATH: You'll be packing me in to one of them homes next. Strapping me in bed for hours in front of telly till my brain goes soft.

GRAHAM: D'yer know how much those places cost?

KATH: Putting my bungalow on market.

37

GRAHAM: Don't give me ideas.

KATH: Your father would be turning / in his grave

GRAHAM: / in his grave? He's bin turnin' in it forty year, I'm surprised he's not come out other side.

ALISON: Dad…

KATH: He knew the value of things. Understood what mattered.

GRAHAM: And he ended up with a son like me. A complete and utter failure.

KATH: Self-pity doesn't suit you.

GRAHAM: What do I wear well, Mum?

KATH: Linda might not understand the importance of this chapel to us but –

GRAHAM: Don't you understand you stupid woman, it's not Linda, I've no bloody money.

A long silence.

BOY appears at the top of the scaffolding. He has made a paper aeroplane. He flies it down to GIRL, who steps out from behind the wall. She picks it up and reads what's written on it.

BOY: What d'yer think?

GIRL: Don't know. Might be busy.

GIRL screws up the paper and puts it into her pocket, smiling.

GRAHAM: *(Softer.)* I can't raise a family on nowt.

KATH: I did.

Pause.

GRAHAM: *(To ALISON.)* Take her home.

KATH: I can take myself.

KATH exits with her stool and placard. GRAHAM sits on the wall. ALISON watches him for a moment. She exits after KATH.

Lights fade.

FOUR

Early Monday morning.

BOY enters nervously smoothing his hair down and adjusting his outfit. He carries a small bunch of dandelions. He breathes on his hand and smells it. He sits at the foot of the wall. GIRL is stood down the side of the chapel, out of BOY's view. Throughout the scene she does her hair several times and attempts to apply lipstick to her mouth and cheeks with her finger.

ALISON enters carrying dust sheets and a toolbox.

ALISON: *(Calling off.)* Thanks to you I spent the whole of Saturday night getting drunk and posting dodgy status updates from the club.

Pause.

Anythin' so I wouldn't have to watch Kim with her tongue down the neck of that poor boy.

Pause.

And I say boy… I swear he was no older than twelve. He was drinking a Smirnoff Ice…

Beat.

…through a straw!

ALISON puts the items down, checks LUCASZ isn't following and quickly rearranges her hair.

And don't try tellin' me yer got carried away in the kitchen again because…

ALISON scoops her left and right boob higher to improve her cleavage.

…Well…

KATH enters, unnoticed. She is wearing a large coat, hat and scarf and is dragging a large selection of miscellaneous items including the placard, a sleeping bag, a flask, food parcels, magazines, and a bag full of letters etc.

(Seeing KATH.) Shit!

She immediately covers her boobs back up.

Sorry you…

KATH: I've never known why men are so fond of them. They're just sacks of fat with a spout. If you got on all fours, they'd be udders.

ALISON: What are you [doin']?

KATH unfolds her stool and sits.

KATH: Fancied a day out.

KATH starts to set up her makeshift station, unpacking various items and placing them around her.

LUCASZ: *(Off.)* I told you. I fell asleep.

LUCASZ enters with a sledgehammer.

KATH: Luke.

ALISON: *(Correcting.)* Lucasz.

LUCASZ: Mrs Bilby.

KATH: There's a bit of your Great Uncle in him.

ALISON: She thinks everyone looks like someone.

KATH: They do after eight decades.

ALISON picks up the sleeping bag.

ALISON: You're not spendin' night?

Beat.

You'll freeze!

LUCASZ: Maybe I should [leave]?

ALISON: This isn't going to change Dad's mind.

KATH: *(Pulling out the sack of letters.)* See how he fares with a flock of us. We might be old, but with age you harden. Like bullets.

ALISON: Who are they?

KATH: You pick people up. I knew more, but they drop like flies.

LUCASZ: You plan revolution? No?

ALISON: No!

A look.

LUCASZ: I'd best…

LUCASZ exits. KATH pushes ALISON's hair off of her forehead.

KATH: Bilby forehead. Intelligent. Like your grandfather. He allus wanted a girl.

ALISON: Bloke who bought it doesn't care. He's just wants the money. I'm sorry. If I could do anything…

KATH hands ALISON the sack.

Oh… I don't…

KATH: There's a postbox round the corner.

ALISON: They don't have stamps.

KATH: They won't mind if it's a good cause.

ALISON: If Dad knew…

KATH: You're a lovely girl.

ALISON hesitates.

ALISON: There's gangs a' kids hang round 'ere at night.

KATH: I'm not scared of a few Teddy Boys. I've not had no trouble in all years.

ALISON: The world's changed. Yer can't –

KATH: I'm eighty-four. I can do as I like.

ALISON exits reluctantly. KATH sits in silence.

GIRL wanders over to BOY.

GIRL: I'm gonna start wettin' the bed if you keep givin' me these.

BOY: Didn't think you were comin'. You got lipstick on?

GIRL: No. Not really… Well. Just a spot.

BOY: Looks nice.

Beat.

I missed yer.

GIRL: Did yer?

BOY: *(Mimicking.)* No. Not really… Well, yeah. Just a spot.

GIRL: If you're goin' t' be like that.

The BOY grabs GIRL's arm and pulls her back down. He kisses her momentarily on the lips and then lets go, embarrassed.

What was that for?

BOY shrugs.

I hope you aint brought me down 'ere t'… 'Cause I won't.

BOY: I just wanted t'see yer again.

GIRL: Why?

BOY: You ask a lot of questions.

GIRL: Nowt wrong wi' bein' curious.

Pause.

I allus see you 'ere. Sittin' starin' over hills. You must be clever. All thinkin' yer do.

BOY: Me dad says I'm either really clever or there's nowt goin' on in there at all. Most of time I'm jus' thinkin' 'bout you.

GIRL: Giv' over.

The BOY is squashing tiny red insects on the floor and looking at the blood on his finger.

BOY: Leave little red dots on your finger.

GIRL: That's blood. You're killin' 'em. My teacher used to say that children who kill animals grow up to be murderers.

BOY: They're not animals. They're insects.

GIRL: Don't think I could ever be wi' a murderer.

BOY: What 'bout you? You've probably sat on about thirty of 'em. That's genocide.

The GIRL leaps up off the floor and frantically starts to brush the back of her dress. The BOY laughs.

GIRL: Next time yer can take me somewhere proper.

BOY: Next time?

Lights fade.

FIVE

Tuesday morning. ALISON and LUCASZ are part way up the scaffolding. They are both wearing cowboy style hard hats.

LUCASZ is holding a Tupperware box full of cupcakes out to ALISON. She takes one, and starts to pick at the icing.

ALISON: *(Looking down at KATH.)* If I was going to sit anywhere, I wouldn't pick 'ere. Would you? Of all buildings t' sit in front of. There's millions of them. All over. In hot places, places with colour. With life. No one's even been into the school room here for years. Last time I did I was seven. Ben locked me in. Scared the shit out of me. So I hit my head again and again on the wall till it freaked him out and he had to open the door. I've still got the scar.

She shows him.

You think we shouldn't do this.

LUCASZ: It's not my decision.

ALISON: They'd just get someone else. Guy's bought places all over the world. Great big stack of them. Hasn't even seen this one. I think yer should have to see somewhere before you buy it. It's like if you eat meat you should be prepared to kill it. He should be here watching Gran die.

LUCASZ: She'll be okay.

ALISON: Not sure dad will.

A text. LUCASZ picks up ALISON's phone.

LUCASZ: Who's Brian?

ALISON: *(Snatching the phone.)* A mate.

Beat.

Like I'd date anyone from round here.

GRAHAM appears, climbing up the scaffold. His hair is dishevelled and he looks tired.

GRAHAM: Yer can start work wi' out me.

ALISON: Elevenses.

GRAHAM: It's ten t' ten.

GRAHAM pours himself a tea from the flask. He downs it.

ALISON: Bad night?

GRAHAM: Try sleepin' wi' a gear stick in your back. Mind, it makes a nice change from yer mother's knee.

He glances at KATH.

See she survived.

ALISON: Yer surprised? Yer wrapped her up like a sausage roll.

GRAHAM: Yeah well…she better not get used to it. I'm not sleepin' in that van forever.

He looks down at KATH. Throughout the rest of the scene he remains fixed on her, only looking away occasionally.

Summat else she's gettin' out for cat.

ALISON: Want some breakfast?

GRAHAM: S'not eatin' flamin' things.

ALISON throws GRAHAM a cupcake.

(To LUCASZ.) We were never gonna make a builder out a' you, were we?

ALISON: Still time.

GRAHAM: Haven't yer told her yet?

ALISON: …

GRAHAM: He's swappin' cement mix for summat a bit sweeter.

LUCASZ: I got the restaurant.

ALISON: In Poland?

GRAHAM: Not greasy spoon down Beetwell Street.

LUCASZ: I want to tell you before but…I think maybe this is bad luck.

ALISON: Amazin'.

She takes a second cupcake and holds it out in cheers.

Another one bites the dust.

She eats quickly, without enjoyment.

GRAHAM: Nice to see someone wi' a bit of nous. Doin' what yer want t' do.

ALISON: You've changed your tune.

GRAHAM: He's worked hard for it.

ALISON: Meaning what?

GRAHAM: You should be happy for him.

ALISON: I am.

GRAHAM: She's givin' it bloody salmon now.

ALISON: S'good t' know this place isn't a black hole.

GRAHAM: Unlike you.

ALISON: Yeah well… Probably have t' pay my next supplier.

Pause.

Guess we should celebrate your release.

LUCASZ: Well…

ALISON: Barkers tomorrow night? I'll bring mates. If I can find any round 'ere who hasn't dropped a sprog.

GRAHAM's phone rings. He looks at the screen and then rejects it.

GRAHAM: *(Suddenly.)* Take them bloody hats off!

LUCASZ takes his hard hat off. ALISON doesn't.

We're builders, not cowboys. Don't know why yer need any.

ALISON: Lucasz's fallen off scaffold three times.

GRAHAM: Then it should've knocked a bit of sense into him.

It starts to spit. GRAHAM holds his palm out and looks up.

Bloody hell!

GRAHAM takes his body warmer off and hands it to LUCASZ.

(Indicating KATH.) An' take her tea an' all. See how long she can cross her legs then.

LUCASZ clumsily exits down the scaffold with the body warmer and flask. ALISON watches him.

That lad's more limbs than he knows what t' do wi'.

Pause.

ALISON: Back to just me an' you.

GRAHAM: He was never much cop. Better t' save money.

ALISON: Christmas party'll be a bit sparse.

GRAHAM: We'll make us own fun. Pass the parcel. Pin the tail on the donkey.

ALISON: No chance.

GRAHAM shakes the rain off his head. ALISON puts LUCASZ's hat on him.

Not so daft now, eh?

They smile.

Yer didn't tell Mum yer were stayin' in van.

GRAHAM: She noticed then?

ALISON: Next time I'll help yer choose perfume. Or at least wrap it.

GRAHAM: Next time I won't bother. Save another bloody row.

ALISON: She sent yer these.

ALISON hands GRAHAM a bag of toiletries. He pulls out a razor.

GRAHAM: Where's she think I'm stayin'?

He drops the razor back into the bag.

ALISON: Missin' home comforts?

GRAHAM: Might not have an en suite but you could fit a
    mattress in back. Be alright t' tour round coast for a few
    weeks. I've allus wanted t' do that.

ALISON: Good luck convincin' Mum.

GRAHAM: No. There'd be too much traffic for her…too many
    crowds…chance of rain.

ALISON: Who's that?

They both look down at where KATH is sitting.

GRAHAM: The crafty…

ALISON: What's he doin'?

GRAHAM: I don't know but he's got a bloody camera.

GRAHAM starts to descend the scaffolding. Lights fade.

SIX

*Tuesday evening. The sound of traffic has been drowned out by the sound
of torrential rain. KATH is sat in her usual position with her handbag
on her lap and the placard standing between the stool and the wall. She
is soaked. GRAHAM stands a few feet away holding a sodden newspaper
over his head.*

*GIRL and BOY are huddled at the side of the scaffolding holding a coat
above both their heads.*

GRAHAM: Let's go home. I'll bring yer back first thing.
    Mum…

KATH looks away.

This place will be death of yer.

KATH: Only thing what keeps me alive.

GRAHAM exits.

GIRL/BOY: *(Singing.)* Are we weak and heavy laden,

Cumbered with a load a' care?

BOY: Stick your head into the oven.
And leave all your troubles there.

GIRL gives BOY a look.

A car horn hoots. KATH waves her hand in dismissal. The car horn sounds again, and this time it is held down.

KATH/GIRL/BOY: *(Singing.)*
Do thy friends despise, forsake thee?
Take it to the Lord in prayer
In his arms he'll take and shield thee.
Thou wilt find a solace there.

Lights fade.

SEVEN

Wednesday lunch. KATH's stool is in the usual place but KATH is not there.

GIRL and BOY are sitting on the wall staring out over the hills.

GIRL: Can't get yer away from this place, can I?

BOY: Best place to concentrate.

GIRL: What on?

BOY: *(Looking at GIRL.)* Scenery.

GRAHAM is standing holding a newspaper. He looks tired and dishevelled.

KATH finally comes on eating a Rich Tea biscuit and carrying a carrier bag with a wet towel and various toiletries. She looks surprisingly refreshed.

GRAHAM: Funny hunger strike.

KATH: It's a Rich Tea.

GRAHAM: If only Gandhi had known they were exempt. You've changed yer clothes.

KATH pulls a wet towel out of her carrier bag and spreads it on the wall to dry.

GRAHAM: Yer've had a shower? Where?

KATH: Yer like an old woman.

GRAHAM: Where?

KATH: Young Charlie's.

GRAHAM: Who the…?

KATH: Number 24. He says it's council but they've a lovely garden.

GRAHAM: I don't believe this.

KATH: He might let you have one. Only you'll have t' wear yer socks because he wasn't sure how his mother would feel about your verruca.

GRAHAM: Bloody Hell.

KATH takes the paper.

KATH: Lovely photo.

GRAHAM: More impressive headline. I'd best tape my letterbox up. What's yer next trick?

KATH: I'm told streaking through the town centre might get me a double-page spread.

ALISON enters with a stack of post and four sausage sandwiches from the local cafe. She is agitated.

ALISON: We need a Portaloo.

GRAHAM: There's pub if yer desperate.

ALISON: Then use it. Or don't leave yer bottle in van.

ALISON hands GRAHAM a sausage sandwich. She hands a second one to KATH, who quickly tucks in, whilst GRAHAM looks on accusingly.

She drops some post on KATH's lap.

GRAHAM: *(Picking one up.)* More cards. Easier for people t' 'think of yer' than join yer.

ALISON: Some flowers were delivered. I left them in your kitchen.

GRAHAM: We'll save them for funeral. Won't be long if yer keep goin' like this.

ALISON goes to exit.

Ali…

ALISON: I've got t' give this t' Lucasz.

GRAHAM: Wait…

ALISON waits.

What's matter?

ALISON: Nothin'.

GRAHAM: Right… Well I –

ALISON: Jo text. She's just moved into her new house. One bed in Nottingham. She's bought it, not rented.

GRAHAM: Good for her.

ALISON: She's havin' an house warming on Friday. Brian's comin' for it. Remember him? He's an illustrator now on this magazine.

GRAHAM: So yer can all share yer good news.

ALISON: What's mine?

GRAHAM: *(Looking at KATH.)* I was gonna wait till things died down…

GRAHAM hands ALISON a business card.

Had them printed up last week.

ALISON: *(Reading.)* Bilby and Daughter.

GRAHAM: Nice ring t' it don't yer think?

KATH: Iscariot and Daughter would've bin more fitting.

ALISON: But Ben…

GRAHAM: Yer brother made decision t' go off an' do his own thing. This is your baby now.

KATH: I'd be asking for more than a name change to do your father's dirty work.

GRAHAM: You've bin here nine –

ALISON: Eight.

GRAHAM: Eight years. Time I showed yer how much I appreciate yer. I'll have name repainted on van. And soon as business improves we'll talk about you havin' some shares. Play us cards right an' this could giv' yer job security for life. We're a good team me an' you.

ALISON: I do yer head in.

GRAHAM: So what d'yer say?

ALISON: I… I don't know.

GRAHAM takes ALISON's hand and shakes it.

GRAHAM: We'll have a ball me an' you Ali. A bloody ball.

Lights fade.

EIGHT

Blackout. The sound of a radio playing the 5 o'clock news fades up.

NEWSREADER: Eighty-four-year-old Kath Bilby has started a protest against the redevelopment of Barrow Hill

Methodist Chapel into a number of luxury one and two-bedroom flats.

(A recording of KATH's voice.) 'My great grandfather collected for years to see this chapel built. At the time, in 1880, this was a poor mining town but everyone gave something. It's been part of the community all these years and we're not going to let it go now.'

NEWSREADER: Messages of support have started pouring in and villagers are turning up to join the fight.

The radio fades out.

NINE

The early hours of Thursday morning. KATH is asleep on the stool, she has been wrapped in sleeping bags. There are lots of empty cups, and extra banners around showing that the place has been bustling. ALISON and LUCASZ enter. They are both tipsy.

BOY and GIRL are lying together on the scaffold, asleep.

ALISON: First time I've had a lock-in there for years. Can't believe Kim didn't last distance.

LUCASZ puts his finger up to indicate he'll be okay in a second.

One more for highway?

ALISON pulls a bottle of Smirnoff Ice out of her pocket.

LUCASZ: *(Seeing KATH.)* Maybe this shortcut was not good idea.

ALISON: After all it's a celebration. You got your fabulous restaurant. And I... I...

LUCASZ shushes her.

(Loud whisper.) I got my life sentence.

LUCASZ holds on to the wall and steadies himself. He looks like he's going to be sick. ALISON grabs his hand and pulls him down beside her.

Dad's on night watch again. Don't know why. He'd sleep through a tsunami. Yer can't take yer drink.

LUCASZ: I can take it. It is the keeping it.

He retches, and then smiles up at ALISON.

ALISON: You even smile when yer vomit. You smiled when you slid off scaffold last year and broke your foot.

LUCASZ: Better than my neck. I see my end. My father said, 'when there is no end, then you are not happy.'

ALISON: I see mine. S'not round 'ere.

ALISON suddenly springs up. She starts to climb the scaffold.

LUCASZ: What are you doing?

ALISON: Testin' freedom.

LUCASZ: Come down, please. You're drunk. Don't make me come up. Not whilst it is moving.

LUCASZ starts to climb after her. ALISON stands at the top of the scaffold and looks out over Barrow Hill.

ALISON: Goes on forever. Maybe I'll keep walkin' till I die. Right way 'round earth. That'd be some life.

LUCASZ: Give me your…

LUCASZ starts to wobble. He grabs the pole with both hands and holds on tightly.

I never try Snakebite again.

ALISON: Wouldn't know where t' go first if I could. America… China…

LUCASZ: The ground.

ALISON starts to waft her arms about.

ALISON: No roofs. Walls. Nobody else 'round me.

She gulps the surrounding air.

I'm inhalin' space. There's loads of it. Nowt t' hold me back.

LUCASZ: Nothing to catch you.

ALISON: I've got you.

Beat.

Haven't I?

LUCASZ: My legs are giving up.

LUCASZ finally grabs hold of ALISON's hand and she allows herself to be led back down the scaffold. LUCASZ slides down the wall.

ALISON: Fancy takin' me with yer?

LUCASZ: You'd bring all the men in to the restaurant.

ALISON: Would I?

Pause.

Don't know. Maybe I'm meant t' stay 'ere. Maybe… Maybe this is…

ALISON suddenly puts her head against her knees and starts to cry.

LUCASZ: Oh no. Ally. No… Shh.

ALISON: How long d'yer get t' escape?

LUCASZ: Never too late.

ALISON: No?

A moment.

God. Sorry. This is supposed t' be a celebration.

LUCASZ: Graham loves you. If you want him to, he'll let you go.

ALISON: Is that why yer wife let you go?

Beat.

Sorry. That's none of my… Too much vodka.

ALISON gives LUCASZ the bottle.

LUCASZ: No I –

ALISON: I wouldn't 'ave let yer go. If yer were my boyfriend I mean. I'd…

She clumsily wraps herself around LUCASZ.

I'd say…you've got to t' get out of that one first.

LUCASZ: *(Gently untangling ALISON.)* It makes me nauseous.

ALISON: Yer never speak about yer wife. Is she – blonde… brunette? Redhead?

LUCASZ: I don't want –

ALISON: No.

LUCASZ: She is just so far away and –

ALISON: Sorry.

LUCASZ: I do not like to / think of her.

ALISON: / S'fine.

Pause.

I should make a move.

LUCASZ: Wait I…

LUCASZ takes a small stone out of his pocket. It has a face drawn on in Tippex. He holds it out to ALISON.

Called Anna.

ALISON takes the stone.

My wife. The stone's just named after her.

LUCASZ shows her a second stone.

And this is Marek.

ALISON: Yer son.

LUCASZ: Always they sit in my pocket. To remind me.

ALISON: *(Studying the stone.)* She's very…

Beat.

Photo's not big back in Poland?

LUCASZ: Sometimes your eye catches a photo and it is so real you think they are actually there. With these, less pain.

ALISON: Here's me goin' on when you're homesick.

Pause. For a moment it is as though they might kiss. The first birdsong of the morning.

God. I hate it when birds sing. Just at peak a' yer tiredness in they come chirpin' away. 'Time's up. Yer missed yer chance.' I'm gonna go.

LUCASZ: I'll walk you.

LUCASZ tries to stand up quickly. The drink hits him.

I might… I might give it a moment.

ALISON exits. LUCASZ slowly slides back down the wall. He watches ALISON leave. He closes his fist around the stones and shuts his eyes. Lights fade.

TEN

A few hours later. KATH is stood by the wall.

BOY and GIRL enter. BOY has his hands over GIRL's eyes. He leads her towards the front of the stage and removes his hands.

BOY: There! I carved it in fence by meself. Used me pocket knife. Do yer like it?

GIRL: I…

BOY: What?

GIRL: Yer've spelt me name wrong.

GIRL climbs up the scaffolding in a huff and sits. BOY goes to follow. GIRL shoots him a look. He sits at the bottom of the scaffolding.

KATH peers over the wall.

KATH: You'll get piles sittin' on a cold floor. Graham gets them sometimes.

LUCASZ appears sleepily from behind the wall. KATH takes a pair of yellow marigolds from her bag and puts them on wearily.

LUCASZ: Where am… Oh… Oh! I'm sorry.

LUCASZ attempts to stand up and tidy himself up.

I had celebration.

KATH retrieves a can of spray paint from her bag. She tries to remove the lid. She fails.

I get carried away. *(He is suddenly overcome by a wave of nausea.)* Urgh!

KATH: Could you?

LUCASZ takes the can and removes the lid.

It was Ernest's job to open things. After he passed on I didn't eat baked beans for years.

LUCASZ holds out the can to KATH.

Says to shake it.

LUCASZ shakes the can and passes it to KATH.

LUCASZ: You are disgusted.

KATH: I've witnessed worse than drink.

LUCASZ: I meant the church.

KATH: S'chapel.

LUCASZ: I want you to know that –

KATH starts to write 'Ernest' on the wall with spray paint.

Shi… Spray paint? Mrs Bilby, I can't let you do that.

KATH: This silly hand.

LUCASZ: If Graham sees that on the… Mrs Bilby… Please. He's only in the car park. I still need this job for a few weeks. My wife's counting on me. My son –

KATH: Can you make / out the name?

LUCASZ: / I beg you /

KATH: / A proper memorial. They're not going to wipe us out.

LUCASZ: Maybe I should go and…

KATH: Ow!

LUCASZ moves towards KATH.

Arthritis. Gets us all in end. *(Attempting to bend down again.)* Ow! This is why people rebel whilst they're young.

KATH holds the can out to LUCASZ.

LUCASZ: Oh… Mrs Bilby. No. I couldn't.

KATH: You'd have liked my husband. He had a soft spot for Poles. Allus listening to Chopin.

LUCASZ: I'm sorry.

Pause.

KATH: Alison says you're going home to start a restaurant.

LUCASZ: Yes. I...

KATH: I expect you're going to have your name over it?

LUCASZ: Wozniac.

KATH: And you want your son to take over someday?

LUCASZ: Five years old and already he's got a set of pots and pans. It is in his blood.

KATH: Something to pass down through generations.

LUCASZ: Yes. Is important. Something I have made. Left behind. Yes. *(With sudden realisation.)* Yes it...

LUCASZ takes the spray can from KATH.

What I put?

KATH takes a lipstick and old receipt from her handbag and writes 'Bilby. 1928-1973.' She hands it to LUCASZ along with the gloves. He puts them on.

I am regretting this already.

KATH: Nice and big.

LUCASZ nervously begins to copy the words onto the wall. As LUCASZ is finishing the last number, GRAHAM enters, rubbing his eyes, as though he has just woken up.

GRAHAM: Lucasz! What the bloody hell do yer think you're doin?!

Lights fade.

ELEVEN

An unspecified time. Night. GIRL is laid on top of the wall. BOY enters.

GIRL: What yer doin' 'ere? They're probably all waitin' t' tear shreds off me. You made me sound like some sort of… And I'm not!

Hesitantly, BOY takes his coat off and places it around GIRL's shoulders.

BOY: Why'd you come here?

GIRL: S'quiet.

BOY: Can't come near 'ere wi'out thinkin' of you.

Pause.

Was a rubbish party. Jimmy snuck some whisky before we left and now he's out cold in bush at back a' hall.

Pause.

I heard yer got wi' him before he passed out.

GIRL: Would hardly have done it after.

BOY stares at GIRL in despair.

BOY: Me dad says it's always pretty girls that are cruellest.

GIRL: What's it matter? We're not together.

BOY: He's me best friend.

GIRL: So?

Beat.

I. Didn't. Get. Wi'. Jimmy.

BOY goes into the pockets of his coat.

Oi.

He pulls out a silver necklace.

Whose is that?

BOY: I got it for yer birthday.

GIRL: But I dumped yer.

BOY: I'd already bought it.

GIRL: It's…

Beat.

I'm so horrible t' yer.

BOY: Dad says that's how you know. If you're willin' t' put up wi' all rubbish then…

GIRL: What?

BOY: S'love.

BOY puts the necklace on GIRL.

GIRL: I didn't…

GIRL kisses BOY on lips. Lights fade.

TWELVE

Thursday afternoon. The fishing stool is stood in the usual place. An opened tub of margarine is lying on the floor. LUCASZ is scrubbing the graffiti off of the wall with a bucket and scrubbing brush.

ALISON enters. She smiles shyly at him, kneels down beside him and takes the spare scrubbing brush.

LUCASZ: You got home okay then?

ALISON: You clearly didn't.

Their arms touch as they both rinse their brush out.

Oh. / Sorry.

LUCASZ: / No I…

They continue scrubbing.

ALISON: Where's Gran?

LUCASZ: Number 24. He already brings her tea and eggs.

ALISON: It's weird. Lad of fourteen.

LUCASZ: He cares.

ALISON: Why? Lads at my school used t' spend any free time thinkin' about girls or stickin' their knobs in curtain rings.

LUCASZ: I didn't.

ALISON smiles.

ALISON: When our science block burnt down, they cheered. Most of 'em still would. We all knew they'd build another one. They always do.

Pause.

I was thinkin' bout last night…

Beat.

No. Not…

GRAHAM enters angrily carrying a bag full of power tools. He holds one up. Its wire has been cut.

GRAHAM: She's hacked through lot a' them. I'll ring her soddin' neck.

ALISON: How d'yer know it was / Gran?

GRAHAM: / Who else'd use nail scissors?

He holds up the offending article.

Take van home before she does owt else.

ALISON: I need t' talk t' yer.

LUCASZ exits.

I'm goin' away.

GRAHAM: Take me wi' yer.

ALISON: I'll stay till we finish this place but then… Are yer listenin'?

GRAHAM: No.

ALISON: I'm serious.

GRAHAM: Yer always are.

ALISON: Yer always find an excuse.

GRAHAM: So what, yer woke up this mornin' an' thought there's got t' be more t' life?

ALISON: Yeah.

GRAHAM: There ain't. I've looked.

ALISON: You've never left England.

GRAHAM: I've heard.

ALISON: I'm suffocatin'. I want t' poke a hole in top a' this box and see some place other than this shit hole.

GRAHAM: I'm sure yer gran would –

ALISON: My life isn't here. I can't keep livin' off crumbs of yours.

GRAHAM: I've just given yer half a' everythin' I have.

ALISON: I know.

GRAHAM: Forty years a' sloggin' me guts out not enough for yer? All you want t' do is slap on a daisy chain and go discover yourself like rest of 'em. Maybe you won't like what yer find.

ALISON: I've eaten, slept and shat in same place for twenty-six years. It hasn't made yer any happier.

GRAHAM: Some a' us can't go swannin' off.

ALISON: Can't or won't?

Pause.

GRAHAM: Go on then. Yer owe me nowt. Wi' any luck I'll drop dead an' then you'll never have t' come back.

ALISON: That's not…

GRAHAM's phone starts to ring. He answers the phone sharply.

GRAHAM: *(Into the phone.)* I've no bloody money.

He hangs up. A pain shoots through his head.

Sod off if yer goin'.

ALISON hesitates and then exits.

Silence.

GRAHAM walks over to the fence and looks into the distance. After a few moments KATH enters. She sits on her stool.

BOY enters pulling GIRL after him.

GIRL: What's rush?

BOY: Told yer, got summat t' ask yer.

GIRL: Couldn't yer ask me back there?

BOY: Can't ask yer nowhere but 'ere.

The GIRL and BOY disappear into the chapel.

After a long time, KATH goes into her handbag and pulls out an array of food, which she sets down on the floor for the cat.

GRAHAM glances at her. He sees the food and turns back around, irritated. KATH starts to make kissing noises.

A look.

KATH: I saw your dad's font. Flung in skip. It's criminal.

GRAHAM: *(He drops the bag of power tools in front of her.)* From one criminal to another.

Silence.

You're a laughin' stock. Where are they all now? A few hours of drinkin' tea and they've gone. Most people still don't even know there was a chapel 'ere.

KATH: They will.

GRAHAM: When you're carted from it in a black box. Or I am.

Pause.

Fifty-six years and what've I got to show for it? Campin' out wi' me bloody mother.

KATH: Then go home.

GRAHAM: I'd rather take me chances wi' you.

The pain shoots through GRAHAM's head again. He holds it. KATH rummages in her bag. She walks over to GRAHAM and pushes a tablet into his ribs.

KATH: Here.

GRAHAM: It'll go in a minute.

KATH: That's what your dad said.

GRAHAM reluctantly takes the tablet. He swallows it without a drink.

Silence. They look out over the fields.

You used to come 'ere when you were a little lad. Never wanted to play out with your friends.

GRAHAM: I never had any.

KATH: Nonsense.

GRAHAM: Only one. That summer when I was about ten, then he left. Remember? His parents moved somewhere up north.

KATH: You used to stand here. Mid-winter, chucking it with rain. Always sketching those gas works. Your father'd allus say, why's he got to draw something so ugly.

Beat.

They've gone now an' all.

A long silence.

GRAHAM: How did we get 'ere, eh?

Silence.

Mum…

Pause.

You and me dad were lucky.

KATH puts her hand on GRAHAM's arm without looking at him. They stand together, like that, for a long time.

Finally, KATH walks back to her stool and picks up the rounders bat from underneath.

What yer doin' wi' that?

Beat.

Eh?

KATH exits into the chapel.

If you touch those… I'll be done. Don't think I'll be stayin' out 'ere watchin' over yer every …

The sound of smashing glass. GRAHAM rushes into the chapel after KATH. Lights fade.

THIRTEEN

Later the same night. The sound of a van leaving. Lights up to a dim glow. BOY and GIRL are sitting on the wall. KATH is sat on her stool.

GIRL: Hands up where I can see them.

BOY: I'm not doin' owt.

GIRL: We're not married yet so you'd best be careful. I've got brothers I have. Billions of them.

A long pause as KATH counts silently on her fingers.

KATH: *(Quietly.)* Adam… John… Matthew… Henry… Harry… Arthur… Pete…

She recounts them silently on her fingers.

Pete… Pete and… I… I can't remember.

She starts to cry gently. The lights start to fade as the sound of teenage voices shouting, laughing and swearing grows louder off-stage.

FOURTEEN

Friday, early morning. The stage is in darkness. GIRL is singing the wedding march. Very slowly the lights rise.

The sign at the front of the church has been defaced so that it now reads 'Kill Methodists'. A pile of cigarette packets and cider bottles litter the floor.

KATH's wrists are tied to the scaffolding and she is barely conscious. She looks like the image of Christ on the cross. She occasionally groans.

GRAHAM rushes in.

GRAHAM: Oh God! Mum! What the hell happened? Mum? C'mon. Open your eyes.

GRAHAM unties the rope quickly and cradles KATH in his lap.

(Calling off-stage.) Tell them t' hurry!

He takes his body warmer off and places it around her.

Look at me. Mum. Open your…

KATH stirs.

Who's done this?

ALISON enters on her mobile phone.

ALISON: Barrow Hill Methodist Chapel. Cavendish Place. Off Station Road. Near the Co-Op. Yes, yes… Okay.

She hangs up. Over the next few lines, ALISON begins to cry silently into her sleeve.

GRAHAM: Why the hell did I go home? I should've stayed.

KATH: They said…they…

GRAHAM: Who did? Mum, who? What low life fuckin' –

ALISON: Dad.

KATH: Dogs… They had –

GRAHAM: If I ever find 'em. I'll rip their bloody… I'll tie 'em t' fuckin…

ALISON: Dad!

KATH closes her eyes again.

GRAHAM: Try t' stay awake. Mum? You're makin' Alison cry.

ALISON: She's not.

GRAHAM: Show her yer okay. Open yer eyes.

KATH: I'm all right.

GRAHAM: Tough ol' boot aren't yer? Take more than this t'get rid a' you.

ALISON: Don't!

GRAHAM: I've tried enough times.

ALISON: No!

GRAHAM: We're just 'avin' a little joke, aren't we Mum? We 'ave us little jokes.

KATH: Yer a good lad.

GRAHAM: Tell Ali about that time me dad dropped me on my head. That's why I've got a bald spot. I'm only thirty.

KATH: Don't... Listen.

GRAHAM: I wouldn't stop crying, so he was bouncing me up and down. Only I slipped right through his hands. Went completely silent for a few seconds. Int that right? They all thought I was dead.

KATH: You screamed.

GRAHAM: That's right. See, stuck wi' each other us two.

KATH: Stuck.

ALISON: She's shiverin'.

GRAHAM: Go get flask of tea.

ALISON exits.

This is over now. It has t' be.

Lights fade.

FIFTEEN

The following week, mid-morning. April. KATH's stool is lying on its side. ALISON and GRAHAM are carrying a large wooden font across the stage.

GRAHAM: Quickly.

ALISON: It's heavy. My hand's / slippin'.

GRAHAM: / Careful!

They carefully lower the font on to the floor.

ALISON: Where's it gonna go?

GRAHAM: We'll find somewhere. Might fit in hall.

ALISON: Mum'll kill yer.

GRAHAM: Yer grandad hand carved that. It's something t' be proud of.

ALISON: You threw it in skip.

GRAHAM: Summat t' pass down the line.

ALISON: Most people pass down somethin' small. A book. Somethin' useful. Suppose it might make a nice bird bath.

GRAHAM: This isn't a... Yer can't get things like this no more. This drew sweat. It means summat.

ALISON: I know.

Silence. ALISON stands KATH's stool back up. She looks at GRAHAM.

GRAHAM: Ready?

He regains his grip on the font and waits for ALISON to join him. She doesn't move.

ALISON: It wasn't your fault...

GRAHAM: Grab the other side.

ALISON: ...what happened with...

GRAHAM lifts the font single-handedly. ALISON quickly grabs onto it.

Yer not responsible for everyone. People can only look after themselves.

GRAHAM: That so?

She steers the font back down.

I was plannin' on doin' other things today yer [know] –

ALISON: I'm still goin'.

Beat.

What happened hasn't changed any... It's worse. If anything. This place it's... I know, I know what you're gonna say and... Don't. For a moment let me just...

Pause.

This is what people do. They leave. I. I have to... I do. I...

GRAHAM: Alison –

ALISON puts her hand up to silence him.

ALISON: Please.

Pause.

I'd like your blessing. More than… I would but… If you can't give it… If I have t' go without…

ALISON notices something behind the wall. She gently lifts the piece of wood up with her foot.

Fuck!

ALISON leaps away from the wall.

Oh…oh shit!

GRAHAM: What?

ALISON: Inside the…

ALISON puts her hand over her mouth as though she is going to gag. GRAHAM looks. Moggy lies there, dead.

GRAHAM: Bloody… Summat's bin at it.

ALISON: Its eyes are still open. Poor…

GRAHAM: No wonder it's not been eating yer gran's food.

ALISON: It could've been there for weeks.

GRAHAM: Only one a' us that's managed t' escape this place.

Silence.

When do yer go?

A look.

ALISON: I… I don't… I haven't…

GRAHAM: Should be able t' get yer booked and packed in a couple of weeks I reckon. Just need t' get yer a flight. Might have t' have a couple of jabs. Depending where you decide t' go.

ALISON: There's…there's no rush.

GRAHAM: Put some brochures for yer in van. I picked them up other night. If yer want them. I wasn't sure where yer were lookin' so…

ALISON: Yeah…no…that's… Thanks.

GRAHAM: They might not be right. I don't really know about / these [things]

ALISON: / Me neither.

GRAHAM: They might give yer some ideas.

Pause.

ALISON: I don't have t' go right away. What with summer comin' prices will be…yer know. And wi' Lucasz leavin' at same time…

GRAHAM: I've builders.

ALISON: Maybe it's best I wait. Just for… For a few months. Till things… I could help yer finish up here. I was thinkin' we could go up coast wi' van. Yer know. I think Mum might come if I –

GRAHAM: No.

ALISON: Could leave in the / Autumn.

GRAHAM: / Yer goin' now and that's that.

Pause.

Bout time me an' yer mum got our love nest back. Yer don't know what she's like when I get her alone. Once upon a time she couldn't keep her hands off me. I used t' have t' fight her off if I brought her down here after dark.

A long pause.

73

ALISON: I'll come back.

GRAHAM: Yer better not.

> *He pats the font.*

> This is going in your room.

> *She smiles at him sadly. Silence.*

> *GRAHAM takes off his jumper.*

> Go get spade.

> *GRAHAM scoops Moggy up in his jumper and cradles him like a baby.*

ALISON: Dad…

> *ALISON hesitates and then exits. GRAHAM sits on KATH's stool, looking down at Moggy who is still in his arms.*

> *Lights slowly fade.*

SIXTEEN

Beginning of May. Monday, afternoon. A huge sign saying 'Show Home Now Open' has been erected.

BOY is sat on the wall. GIRL enters and walks up to him. BOY doesn't respond. GIRL sits down next to him.

GIRL: You can't keep disappearing like this.

> *Beat.*

> We're married now. We need t' stick together.

BOY: He's been lookin' for an excuse t' fire me for months.

GIRL: Yer lost yer job?

BOY: Not sure I could've stood him much longer.

GIRL: We need it.

BOY: We'll be fine. We've your wage.

Beat.

What?

GIRL: I handed me notice in today. It was going t' be a surprise.

BOY: Why hell d'you do that? Get it back.

GIRL: They already took somebody on.

BOY: So quick? Yer knew situation when you married me. I never pretended t' have more than I 'ave.
I wish yer didn't 'ave t' work but yer do.

Beat.

I want t' be on me own.

GIRL: Please –

BOY: Something's got into yer lately.

GIRL: Yeah?

BOY: And you'd best get it back out.

GIRL: Give it nine months.

A look.

BOY: What?

Beat.

You're not…?

She smiles.

That's…that's… How long yer known?

GIRL: Couple a' weeks.

BOY: A couple a'…

BOY kisses the GIRL enthusiastically.

I can't believe it. You're… Somewhere in there is our …

75

GIRL: What about money?

BOY: I'll start grovellin' Monday.

BOY takes GIRL's hand and makes to move.

GIRL: Where we goin'?

BOY: I'm plannin' on shoutin' it from rooftops.

GIRL: You get head start. I want a second. Catch my breath before it all starts.

BOY starts to run off. Stops. Runs back and kisses GIRL. He exits.

KATH enters. Her hair is unruly and for the first time she looks dishevelled. She is holding a Morrisons carrier bag. She stands and looks at the chapel.

GRAHAM enters, on the phone.

GRAHAM: Au revoir. No, I know you're not but I can't speak Russian. Go on then. Go and have a… You'll be fine. Yeah? Okay. I'd best [go]… Bye then. Yeah. Bye… Bye…

He waits, listening.

Ali?… You'll be fine… Okay. We'll speak soon. Bye. Bye.

He waits a moment and then hangs up.

I told her not to ring for a few days. It seems to make her worse.

KATH looks around for Moggy. She sees the water carton has been kicked in to the corner and picks it up.

It'll have found a new home. Someone as daft as you. It'll be on a warm lap somewhere.

KATH makes half-hearted kissing noises to attract the cat.

It's probably got itself in to one a' new flats. Be watching a Whisker's ad on a 44-inch flat screen. Have you seen inside one? They've all mod cons. Power showers, those spa baths. I'm sure someone'll let us have a look round if…

KATH has taken a meringue out of the carrier bag and is holding it out as a temptation for the cat.

KATH: Moggy…

GRAHAM: We don't have t' rush. I'm not pickin' Linda up till nine. She's started an exercise class – god knows what they do in it for hours. I brought camera. Thought I could get a few shots. Ben was gonna do yer a little website. Anything you want me to take?

KATH doesn't respond.

One a' front?

GRAHAM holds his camera up to take the shot. As he does so, GIRL stands. For the first time, both KATH and GRAHAM see her. GRAHAM slowly pulls his camera down. They both watch her, transfixed.

Finally GIRL disappears into the flats. A sudden emptiness hangs in the air.

KATH: Take me away.

KATH exits, dropping the meringue as she goes.

GRAHAM stands still for a long time before very slowly following KATH out. He glances back momentarily.

The lights slowly fade out.

WWW.OBERONBOOKS.COM

 Follow us on www.twitter.com/@oberonbooks
& www.facebook.com/oberonbook